PROMISED TREASURES

DAILY DEVOTIONS

REV. DR. TIMOTHY R. PULS

CONCORDIA PUBLISHING HOUSE · SAINT LOUIS

ASH WEDNESDAY AND THE DAYS FOLLOWING

Covered in Ashes

Read Job 2:1–8

And he took a piece of broken pottery with which to
scrape himself while he sat in the ashes. (Job 2:8)

As we enter Lent, we seek to be mindful of our sins. However, we are more cognizant of their weight, causing death for God's entire creation, which groans and longs for eternal redemption (see Romans 8:19–22). From our viewpoint, Job did not deserve what occurred to him. We know what took place behind the scenes when the Lord and Satan conferred (see Job 1–2), but Job knew none of it before he suffered. Pain is never fully explained in the immediate. That is why Job just scraped his sores and boils with a piece of pottery and sat in ashes. In significant grief, only supportive words, regular prayers, and godly counsel help.

Are you covered in ashes, shattered by a diagnosis of cancer or news of the death of a family member? Sickness, death, and brokenness are realities now, as Jesus says: "In the world you will have tribulation" (John 16:33). However, remember what He says after: "But take heart; I have overcome the world." Jesus Christ overcomes every pain, grief, and anxiety because He died and rose for you. Since all your troubles are His, remember that He sympathizes with you (see Hebrews 4:15), giving to you the strength of the Spirit for life today and the promise of the resurrection of the body for the life to come.

Lord Jesus, assure me that You are always with me,
even in my dust and ashes of life. Amen.

Who Will Help Me from My Ashes?

Read Job 19:23–27

For I know that my Redeemer lives, and at the last
He will stand upon the earth. And after my skin has
been thus destroyed, yet in my flesh I shall see God.
(Job 19:25–26)

The life of the baptized is often a daily, fickle journey from unbelief to faith. Job wallows in ashes one day (see Job 2) but makes a marvelous confession the next (Job 19): "I Know That My Redeemer Lives" (*LSB* 461). St. Peter boldly confessed, "You have the words of eternal life" (John 6:68) and "You are the Christ, the Son of the living God" (Matthew 16:16), yet he tried to deter Jesus from the cross (see Matthew 16:22) and denied Him three times (see Matthew 26:69–75).

This helps us understand why one man said to Jesus, "I believe; help my unbelief!" (Mark 9:24). Dr. Luther says, "[Holy Baptism] indicates that the Old Adam in us should by daily contrition and repentance be drowned and die with all sins . . . and that a new man should daily emerge and arise to live before God" (Small Catechism, "What Baptism Indicates," Part 4). Even when your old man wins one day, do not look inwardly to improve! Rather, die in ashes, confess your sin, and rise again in Jesus. Through the rosy-red waters of Holy Baptism, Jesus washes you by His cross, now and always!

Lord Jesus, I believe. Help my unbelief, that I may
confess You as my Savior and Redeemer all my days.
Amen.

Repentance with Ashes

Read Matthew 11:20–30

Then [Jesus] began to denounce the cities where most
of His mighty works had been done, because they did
not repent. (Matthew 11:20)

After Adam and Eve sinned, God immediately pronounced the Law to the serpent (the devil). The Seed (Jesus) of the woman (Mary) would crush the serpent's head (Satan; see Genesis 3:15 NIV) at the cross. The crushing of Satan's head is the full strength of God's wrath, but it proves to be the Good News for mankind. Adam and his descendants can only survive the burden of sin by hearing that the serpent will be crushed. However, after those words of hope for mankind, God gave Adam Law: "By the sweat of your face you shall eat bread, till you return to the ground, for out of it you were taken; for you are dust, and to dust you shall return" (Genesis 3:19).

Lent announces the Law as dust and ashes are smeared on our foreheads. None of us can escape death because the cause, sin, still dwells within. Such sobering words are worth hearing. Thanks be to God that the heavenly Father reveals this to us, His little children. Even though the reality of sin and death does not affect the wise Chorazins and learned Bethsaidas of this world, who see and hear what Christ has done but reject it, it is revealed to you. Thank God for your dust and ashes, for they drive us to Jesus, who says, "Come to Me, all who labor and are heavy laden, and I will give you rest. . . . And you will find rest for your souls" (Matthew 11:28–29).

Lord Jesus, come to me, for I am weary and burdened.
Give rest to my soul. Amen.

A Beautiful Headdress Instead of Ashes

Read Isaiah 61:1–4

To grant to those who mourn in Zion—to give them a beautiful headdress instead of ashes, the oil of gladness instead of mourning. (Isaiah 61:3)

Before Adam and Eve were banished from Eden, the Lord made and gave them garments of skin that they should be covered by His grace (see Genesis 3:21–24). *Unclothing* and *clothing* are common baptismal words describing life as God's children. St. Paul spends extensive time talking about "putting off" sin, anger, wrath, malice, and lying. Then, he encourages us to "put on" compassion, kindness, brotherly love, and, above all, forgiveness (Colossians 3).

Sadly, our hearts and minds are often filled with negative and evil thoughts toward others and ourselves (see Matthew 15:19). Therefore, we cannot simply jump from hate to love. I must die and be buried each morning. When I can hear or reflect on God's Word and receive His Sacraments, then I rise anew, today and every day. Since Jesus Christ died, was buried, and rose again, all for you, every day is a new Easter! As St. Paul says, "For you have died, and your life is hidden with Christ in God" (Colossians 3:3). Covered with new skin and a beautiful headdress, you are concealed in the blood of Jesus, God's Son, and are washed in Him. You do not need to walk in ashes any longer, but when you do, remember to wash and repeat, unclothe and reclothe!

Dear Jesus, clothe me anew in kindness, compassion, and love for all. Amen.

LENT
WEEK ONE

Dust and Ashes Breathed New Life

Read Ezekiel 37:1–14

Thus says the Lord GOD to these bones: Behold, I
will cause breath to enter you, and you shall live.
(Ezekiel 37:5)

When God created the heavens and the earth (see Genesis 1), He brought everything "out of nothing," *ex nihilo* as the Latin translates it. We confess with our lips this truth in the Nicene Creed: "I believe in one God, the Father Almighty, maker of heaven and earth and of all things visible and invisible." God repeats creation in Ezekiel's vision of dry bones. Life is often a lifeless, dusty desert, and filled with death, like skeletons at Halloween. Here, the Lord told Ezekiel to prophesy directly to the dry bones, and suddenly life sprang forth. A rattling sound came first as bones snapped back together, new sinews twisted around the joints, and new flesh covered all these bodies. Finally, Ezekiel prophesied to the breath, and life came to this great army.

Are you sitting in a dry, lifeless desert today? Does life's closet have too many dry bones of sin and bad decisions? No matter how dry life is, today is Sunday, always a day of resurrection.

Rejoice now because Jesus and His forgiveness fill you with hope and peace and breathe new life on you.

Dear Lord Jesus, raise these dry bones by Your Word
and the work of the Holy Spirit so that I may rise anew
with joy, purpose, and meaning. Amen.

You Are the Salt of the Earth

Read Matthew 5:13–16

You are the salt of the earth, but if salt has lost its taste,
how shall its saltiness be restored? (Matthew 5:13)

Jesus' death on Calvary's cross not only washes all our sins away but also thoroughly scours, cleans, and vaccinates the world from its power to condemn. Salt was a cleansing, healing, and preserving commodity in the ancient world. By it, bodily wounds were disinfected and meat and food were preserved for days or weeks at a time. Salt, therefore, was valuable in many ways!

Now, Jesus calls you the salt of the earth. Your life tastes different from the world because the blood of Jesus cleanses, separates, washes, and preserves you with joy wherever you go. That began in your Baptism. This is why the earliest baptismal rites often included a small taste of salt placed on the lips. This reminded the Church that all new Christians are salted and seasoned by Christ! This is probably why even Martin Luther retained it in his first rite of Baptism in 1523.[1] Remember today that you are precious to God, distinctly preserved with the salt of wisdom and grace through God's Holy Word.[2] As His precious child and eternally adopted heir, your life preserves, strengthens, and seasons others with life all around you (see Ephesians 1:3–14)!

> Lord Jesus, You made us salt of the earth. Preserve my
> life today that I may bring the seasoning of love, hope,
> and peace to all I see and meet. Amen.

---

[1]   Helmet T. Lehman, ed., *Luther's Works, Liturgy and Hymns* (Fortress Press: Philadelphia, 1965), 53:98.

[2]   E. C. Whitaker, *Documents of the Baptismal Liturgy,* 2nd ed. (London, 1970), 155.

Too Much Salt

Read Psalm 107:28–38

He turns rivers into a desert, springs of water into
thirsty ground, a fruitful land into a salty waste.
(Psalm 107:33)

Although the ocean is full of salt water, freshwater rivers and rain bring the earth balance. If water is overly salty, life cannot exist. At one of the lowest elevations on earth, the Dead Sea is one such place. Fresh water flows into it from the Jordan, but since it cannot flow out, it is overly salty, quelling life for all fish and plants. Salt must be balanced in your body as well. A healthy amount of sodium keeps your body fit and healthy. Too much sodium, however, may cause high blood pressure, and low sodium, often depleted through exercise, may cause your muscles to fail to work. This is why energy drinks are popular. They add electrolytes (or salt) back into your body.

God always provides you, His baptized child in Christ, with the right amount of salt through regular reception of His Word and Sacraments so that you may taste salty to others while not being a salty waste. By Jesus' death and resurrection, you are preserved from sin, death, and hell. And while you yet remain in this world, your saltiness may be a blessing to others.

Lord Jesus, You have made us the salt of the earth in
Holy Baptism. Let our lives reflect Your life in us now
and always. Amen.

Sweetened by Salt

Read 2 Kings 2:19–21

Then [Elisha] went to the spring of water and threw
salt in it and said, "Thus says the LORD, I have healed
this water; from now on neither death nor miscarriage
shall come from it." (2 Kings 2:21)

Have you ever heard of salt sweetening? Some people place salt on watermelon or tomatoes to accentuate their sweet flavor. However, salt does not normally sweeten. Yet God allowed Elisha to perform a miracle with only a pinch of salt. He restored stagnant, deathlike water into fresh springs for people to drink.

Is there anything sour stagnating in your life, your health, or in that of a loved one? Do you have any bitter relationships with people? Is your vocation or work stressful or unsatisfying? In all of life's tainted experiences, Jesus Christ, your Savior, knows and sympathizes with them all (see Hebrews 4:15). In human flesh, He endured all of life to be your advocate and intercessor. This Lent, remember again that He died on Calvary's cross so that, like salt that sweetens, we have the assurance that even the deepest wounds of life are but momentary afflictions. The Lord is not distant from you. Rather, He heals, delivers, and sustains you in all your troubles (see Psalm 34). "The LORD is near to the brokenhearted and saves the crushed in spirit" (Psalm 34:18).

Lord Jesus, in my troubles, invigorate me by the Holy
Spirit with salt to preserve and sweeten life in the midst
of my pain. Amen.

Salt-Seasoned Speech

Read Colossians 4:2–6

Let your speech always be gracious, seasoned with salt,
so that you may know how you ought to answer each
person. (Colossians 4:6)

One of my favorite things is to barbecue. I will often season meat with a rub and allow it to sit for an hour before grilling it. Premade rubs are so popular because special seasonings accent different meats in unique ways. However, the main ingredient in most rubs is salt because it seasons and improves taste.

How does your speech taste to those closest to you? Is it gently seasoning others with encouragement, joy, and peace, or is it oversalted with filthy talk, criticism, and angry words? The biggest impression you leave with others often comes through words. St. Paul says, "Walk in wisdom toward outsiders. . . . Let your speech always be gracious, seasoned with salt" (Colossians 4:5–6). Jesus was often tempted to spout angry, resentful words, yet there was never a word of deceit in His mouth (1 Peter 2:22). Jesus makes your life and speech new every day because you died with Him on the cross. Salted in Him by Baptism, you are raised with resurrection power to crucify the old speech so that new words encourage everyone around you.

> Lord Jesus, when I am tempted to criticize and speak
> unhelpful, useless words, please season my speech
> with salt, that I may praise You and encourage others.
> Amen.

Salted in Covenant

Read Leviticus 2:11–16

You shall season all your grain offerings with salt. You shall not let the salt of the covenant with your God be missing from your grain offering; with all your offerings you shall offer salt. (Leviticus 2:13)

Salt was required with every grain offering in the Old Testament. The grain offerings were first portions of vegetables or grain offered to God alone by the people of Israel. This reminded them that as God kept His covenant with Abraham, so He was keeping it with them as well.

Do you know that you are the Lord's forever as well? You are also a child of Abraham, baptized into Christ and now called the salt of the earth. Even though your present body is infected by sin and death, it will be preserved for all eternity. After Jesus rose from the dead, He called His disciples His brothers and His Father our Father. Let that promise fill you with hope today! Even though your present body is limited by sin, sickness, and age, you will have a new resurrected body without any of the present limitations through the risen Christ. When you are laid to rest someday, remember that temporal death does not last forever! When Christ comes to raise all the dead, all those salted, or baptized, into Christ will live forever (1 Corinthians 15).

> Dear Lord Jesus, thank You for salting me in Holy Baptism, promising me that this temporal body will rise to eternal life someday. Amen.

Salted through Song

Read Acts 16:25–34

Let the word of Christ dwell in you richly, teaching
and admonishing one another in all wisdom, singing
psalms and hymns and spiritual songs, with thankful-
ness in your hearts to God. (Colossians 3:16)

Imagine the jailer's terror after an earthquake struck the jail in Philippi the first night Paul and Silas were in prison. Since the jail was now open for all prisoners to escape, and the jailer would be held to account for their escape, he almost committed suicide. However, Paul halted him. Then the jailer asked, "Sirs, what shall I do to be saved?" He was salted and seasoned by the singing of hymns and prayers to God from Paul and Silas. He wanted Jesus, the source of eternal life, and that night his whole family was baptized and saved as well.

One of my late seminary professors often encouraged his students to memorize Scriptures and hymn stanzas. There is nothing like approaching someone's bedside and then singing a hymn. The sick one, and others gathered around, are drawn in and encouraged to look outside themselves. In that singing, they are confronted with a God who still cares, loves, and preserves at all times, even at the approach of death. Your saltiness in word and song literally makes you hopeful, joyful, and attractive to any who see or hear you.

> On my heart imprint Your image,
> Blessed Jesus, King of grace,
> That life's riches, cares, and pleasures
> Never may Your work erase;
> Let the clear inscription be:
> Jesus, crucified for me,
> Is my life, my hope's foundation,
> And my glory and salvation (LSB 422)! Amen.

LENT
WEEK TWO

Led by Still Waters

Read Psalm 23

The LORD is my shepherd; I shall not want.
He makes me lie down in green pastures.
He leads me beside still waters. (Psalm 23:1–2)

How refreshing is a glass of ice water on an extremely hot day? Very refreshing! The "still waters" that King David describes are often an image of peace, serenity, and refreshment. As a gentle shepherd leads lambs to fresh water to drink and green pastures to lie down, God always sustains, refreshes, and nourishes His people. "As a deer pants for flowing streams, so my soul pants for You, O God" (Psalm 42:1). God never rejects thirsty people; He always hears when they cry to Him (see Psalm 34). Jesus probably heard the cry of the Samaritan woman before she arrived at the well and received living water.

Today, Sunday, is your day of rest and refreshment with all of God's people. He gives us forgiveness and love to refresh, encourage, and uplift us along life's way. In every week's dry desert, Jesus offers you Himself, an eternal well of living water (see John 4:14). "If anyone thirsts, let him come to Me and drink" (John 7:37). The one that drinks the water only Jesus gives will never thirst again!

> Lord Jesus, I am thirsty and need something to drink! I am restless and anxious, needing peace. Bless me today by Your Word and Spirit that I may have joy and peace. Amen.

Saved by Flooding Water

Read Genesis 8:1–7, 13–19

At the end of forty days Noah opened
the window of the ark that he had made. (Genesis 8:6)

Is this an oxymoron? There is life after flooding! Every year there is destruction from hurricanes, floods, and tornadoes. However, none is as deadly as the worldwide flood that occurred in the days of Noah. This was the greatest loss of human life ever recorded. Nothing with the breath of life survived unless it was within Noah's ark. All life, except all the fish and creatures in the water, was extinguished.

However, God brought new life for Noah and his family to enjoy. They even set foot on dry land again. Human sinful flesh, the power of this dark world, and the deception of the devil are still the deadliest powers threatening us. Yet this is why the flooding waters of Baptism must still pour over you every day. There, an old you dies with Christ on the cross, is drowned and buried with Him, so that a new you is resurrected and reborn by Jesus. Your sinful flesh will exist as long as your heart is beating, but know that you are washed by the blood of Jesus, and by Him, you serve the living God.

> Lord Jesus, I am stuck in the mire of my sin. Drown my
> sinful flesh by the power of Your crucifixion so that I
> may live anew today. Amen.

In the Lord's Navy

Read 1 Peter 3:18–22

Baptism, which corresponds to this [the ark, Noah,
and his family], now saves you, not as a removal of
dirt from the body, but as an appeal to God for a good
conscience, through the resurrection of Jesus Christ.

(1 Peter 3:21)

Do you like boats? There is nothing like floating above a glistening body of water on a beautiful sunny day. As a baptized child of God, you float too, redeemed in the blood of Jesus, above the flood of sin and death. Although your body is subject to sin, death, and decay, you are not anchored to an eternal, tormenting death in hell. No, you will be carried by God's holy angels to the shores of heaven and Abram's bosom (see *LSB* 708:3). With Jesus Christ as your pilot, you no longer fear judgment or His glorious coming.

Many congregations illustrate our floating life in Baptism by the design of their church, especially the area where people sit, called the "nave." The Latin word *nav* is where we get the English word *navy*. You are safe in God's ship of Holy Baptism. Just as US Navy ships protect this country, so the ark of Christ's Church keeps you buoyant, secured, and saved from all dangers outside the boat.

> Jesus, Savior, pilot me
> Over life's tempestuous sea;
> Unknown waves before me roll,
> Hiding rock and treach'rous shoal.
> Chart and compass come from Thee.
> Jesus, Savior, pilot me (*LSB* 715:1). Amen.

Born of Water and the Spirit

Read John 3:1–21

Jesus answered, ". . . Unless one is born of water and
the Spirit, he cannot enter the kingdom of God."
(John 3:5)

Nicodemus was a distinguished member of the Jewish ruling council, the Sanhedrin. He was stunned, shocked, and dumbfounded when Jesus told him the night he snuck in to visit Him that he, already born of Abraham, also must be given another birth to enter the kingdom of God. He sarcastically asked, "How can a man be born when he is old? Can he enter a second time into his mother's womb and be born?" (John 3:4). The obvious answer is no!

Oh, how the Church knows the pains of labor. Though the labor is intense, she knows that those who by the water of Baptism go through the death of the flesh are by the Spirit born into life in Christ. The labor involved in spiritual rebirth, being born of water and the Spirit, requires the death and drowning of sinful flesh. Yet by it comes access into the Church and God's kingdom. God saves you by His Holy Spirit through His Son, Jesus, who died to save you. While all people have a fleshly birth, not all have been spiritually born in Holy Baptism. Here, by the Spirit, and in Christ's Church, you are certain of your new birth in the name of the Father, and of the Son, and of the Holy Spirit.

> Here we bring a child of nature;
> Home we take a newborn creature,
> Now God's precious son or daughter,
> Born again by Word and water (*LSB* 593:4). Amen.

In the Potter's Hands

Read Jeremiah 18:1–12

But now, O Lord, You are our Father;
we are the clay, and You are our potter;
we are all the work of Your hand. (Isaiah 64:8)

My eighth-grade teacher once gave my class an art project to make our own piece of clay pottery. The first and foremost step when working with the clay was to keep it moist. If the clay lost its moisture, you would have to start all over because the clay would not bind together. The final warning issued to all the students was this: Do not fire the clay until you have completely finished it. I learned that clay is pliable when moistened by water, but once fired, the pot is complete.

When God told Jeremiah to go to the potter's house, He showed him how His people were dried-out and fired clay. Jeremiah even broke a piece of pottery in front of Israel to illustrate how they had rebelled and rejected God. This Lent, we need the same. Dried by sin and hardened by our sinful world, we are depleted of living water. But your heavenly Father never forsakes His promises. He forgives and loves you every day, reshaping you like fresh moistened clay with baptismal water into the image of His Son, Jesus.

> Heavenly Father, by Your Spirit, reshape me into the
> image of Your Son, Jesus. Drown my old Adam so that I
> may rise with joy to serve You. In Jesus' name. Amen.

Which Water and How Much?

Read 2 Kings 5:1–14

Jesus said to him, "The one who has bathed does not
need to wash, except for his feet, but is completely
clean. And you are clean, but not every one of you."
(John 13:10)

The love of God is expansive in the washing of Naaman, the leprous commander of Syria's army. A captive Israelite girl told Naaman's wife that Elisha, who was in Israel, could heal him. However, he balked at Elisha's word before eventually dipping into the Jordan River seven times. Peter also balked when Jesus offered to wash his feet. Pride could have gotten the better of each man, preventing Naaman's skin from being healed and Peter from having any share with Jesus, much like Judas.

Never allow your sinful old man to belittle God's awesome promises in your Baptism. Even if you do not remember it because you were a baby, that does not negate Baptism's effect or power. Additionally, neither the kind nor the amount of water is the power for Baptism. All God's promises of His Holy Word, which *is* the power of Baptism, were packed into the water in your Baptism, no matter where or when it took place! Take heart, as did Naaman and Peter, who heard the Word, believed, and were washed. All your sins are forgiven in Jesus, the gift of the Holy Spirit is yours, and you are an heir of heaven.

> Dear Lord Jesus, forgive me for my pride. Thank You
> for washing me in Holy Baptism of all my sin, giving
> me eternal life. Amen.

Thirsting for God

Read Exodus 17:1–7

On the last day of the feast, the great day,
Jesus stood up and cried out, "If anyone thirsts,
let him come to Me and drink." (John 7:37)

After God brought ten plagues on Egypt and Israel safely crossed the Red Sea, the Israelites soon grumbled. They complained to God and Moses because there was no water to drink. Each year, Israel celebrated Passover and the Festival of Booths (living in tents) so that they would never forget how well God provides for His people. Although Israel lived in tents for forty years, God provided daily manna, water, and clothing, and their sandals never wore out. It was on this festival, then, that Jesus offered Himself as the living water.

Do you ever find yourself grumbling? Is life not going the way you think it should? It is easier to blame others, forget God, and grumble and complain. However, remember what God gives you every day. He gives you all your daily bread, including clothing, shelter, and so much more. Jesus says, "If anyone thirsts, let him come to Me and drink." Drink deeply of all the living water, finding all your sustenance in Jesus, who made you and forgives you through the precious living water of your Baptism. His well is never dry! Thirst no more!

Dear Lord Jesus, forgive me when I grumble about my
life and Your provision. Draw me, again, to the waters
and promises of Holy Baptism. Amen.

LENT
WEEK THREE

Let There Be Light

Read 2 Corinthians 4:5–6

And God said, "Let there be light," and there was light.
And God saw that the light was good. (Genesis 1:3–4)

Light is a created phenomenon in God's creation. For when God created the world, "darkness was over the face of the deep" (Genesis 1:2). God ushered light into His world out of nothing, then He separated light from darkness. Later, God made formal lights in the expanse of the heavens—the sun, the moon, and the stars—to separate day and night and provide signs and seasons, creating time itself (see Genesis 1:16).

After the Creator of the world, Jesus (see John 1:1), was incarnated, He called Himself the light of the world (see John 8:12). Anyone who follows Him is no longer in the dark. Sadly, many people are vexed by darkness, assuming that light is found in numerous places. They are sadly mistaken! Your Eternal Light was crucified and bloodied on a cross! He died and was buried in darkness, but He rose again in light. Outside of Him, there is no light (see John 14:6). Thank God for revealing the light of Jesus to you, making you a child of the light in Holy Baptism. To have Jesus is to have eternal light and life.

> O Christ, our true and only light,
> Enlighten those who sit in night;
> Let those afar now hear Your voice
> And in Your fold with us rejoice (*LSB* 839:1). Amen.

I Am the Light of the World

Read Psalm 27

I am the light of the world. Whoever follows Me will
not walk in darkness, but will have the light of life.
(John 8:12)

Have you ever been in a pitch-black room or cave? If so, then you have felt the darkness press upon you. The news of sin and darkness in our world often dampens hope, making the prospect of your future depressing. Additionally, the myriad of sinful thoughts, anxieties, and pangs of conscience that hit you can make life gloomy.

King David shares a marvelous promise in Psalm 27, bringing comforting words of light and wisdom: "The LORD is my light and my salvation; whom shall I fear? The LORD is the stronghold of my life; of whom shall I be afraid?" (v. 1). After darkened Pharisees press Jesus, He tells them that when He is lifted up on the cross, then they will know that He has been sent from the Father. Remember, this Lent, that God shields you from all the harming effects of darkness because Jesus went to the cross for you. When you cry aloud in pain or darkness, know that He is your rock, stronghold, and shield. He hears your voice (see Psalm 27:7; 34:15).

> Light of Light, O Sole Begotten
> Radiance of the Father's face,
> Word made flesh, who lived among us
> Full of truth and full of grace,
> Shine upon our human darkness;
> Pierce the night that shrouds our race (*LSB* 914:1).
> Amen.

Bright Lampstands

Read Exodus 37:17–24

Then I turned to see the voice that was speaking to me,
and on turning I saw seven golden lampstands, and in
the midst of the lampstands one like a son
of man, clothed with a long robe and with
a golden sash around His chest. (Revelation 1:12–13)

Candles are usually plentiful in churches because they have a rich, biblical root. Bezalel, a fine artisan in the days of Moses, hammered out the first sevenfold lampstand of pure gold (see Exodus 37:17). It resembled an almond plant with branches, blossoms, and flowers. The lamps were always lit within the tabernacle and temple, the holy place where God dwelled among His people. Lamps are mentioned in the parable of the ten virgins with lamps and oil (see Matthew 25:1–13) and in Revelation. The seven lampstands correlate with the seven churches where Jesus Christ, the Son of Man, dwells in their midst (see Revelation 1–3).

Candles often symbolize God's presence with us in His Word and Sacraments. They fill us with light and hope even during the dark season of Lent, promising that Jesus Christ is with us with all His love, joy, forgiveness, peace, and power. Baptized into Him, the light of the world, you are never without hope or purpose, and His light is never hidden.

Dear Lord Jesus Christ, the light of the world, remove
the gloom of sin and darkness from me, that I may
reflect Your light, love, and joy wherever I go. Amen.

Children of the Light

Read Ephesians 5:1–15

Therefore be imitators of God. . . . And walk in love, as Christ loved us and gave Himself up for us, a fragrant offering and sacrifice to God. . . . Now you are light in the Lord. Walk as children of light. (Ephesians 5:1–2, 8)

Jesus calls you "the light of the world" (Matthew 5:14), and St. Paul calls you "children of light" (Ephesians 5:8). What does that mean for you as a baptized child of God? It means that you humbly realize that at one time, you, too, were dead and purposeless without God. However, since Christ loved you, as Lent illustrates, laying down His life, shedding His precious blood on the altar of the cross as a fragrant burnt offering, your life now is completely different and new.

Now you reflect His light. Rather than participating in the deeds of darkness, you expose them, especially sexual immorality, covetousness, and all filthy talk (see Ephesians 5:3–7). That must be done carefully, lovingly, and compassionately, bearing fruit in all that is good and right and true (see Ephesians 5:9). Do not avoid the truth, but lovingly reflect the One who forgives you all your sins and makes you light in this world. Baptized into Him, you are light wherever you go in this world.

> Take my life and let it be
> Consecrated, Lord, to Thee;
> Take my moments and my days,
> Let them flow in ceaseless praise (*LSB* 783:1). Amen.

Oil in Your Lamp and More

Read Matthew 25:1–13

Thus says the LORD, the God of Israel, "The jar of flour
shall not be spent, and the jug of
oil shall not be empty, until the day that the LORD
sends rain upon the earth." (1 Kings 17:14)

The problem for the widow at Zarephath during Elijah's day and for half the virgins in Jesus' parable is the lack of oil. The widow only had enough for one more meal with her son before they would die from the effects of a severe drought. Likewise, the foolish virgins in Jesus' parable only had enough oil in their lamps for part of their journey to the marriage feast, but they neglected to gather more.

Do you ever feel a little like the widow at Zarephath, with seemingly no way to provide for yourself or others? On the other hand, do you feel like the foolish virgins, knocking helplessly on the door of the banquet hall, knowing you have failed? God knows every trouble, anxiety, and pain. He promises you more than enough oil through His gracious Word and Sacraments to sustain and save you (see Psalm 34:6, 17, 19). Baptized into Jesus Christ, the Anointed One, all your anxieties are His. So arise with new light, hope, and joy. As Isaiah says, "A bruised reed He will not break, and a faintly burning wick He will not quench" (Isaiah 42:3).

> Renew me, O eternal Light,
> And let my heart and soul be bright,
> Illumined with the light of grace
> That issues from Your holy face (*LSB* 704:1). Amen.

Two Candles, One Christ

Read Colossians 1:15–20

For in Him the whole fullness of deity dwells bodily.

(Colossians 2:9)

During Lent, it is easy to forget that the God of the universe was openly betrayed by Judas, publicly denied by Peter, and falsely charged with blasphemy. Beyond this, He was mocked, punched, and spit upon before He was marched to Calvary. This suffering, however, was not endured by an ordinary man, but, as St. Paul confesses, "He is the image of the invisible God. . . . For in Him all the fullness of God was pleased to dwell, and through Him to reconcile to Himself all things, whether on earth or in heaven, making peace by the blood of His cross" (Colossians 1:15, 19–20).

If you ever forget who Jesus Christ is, remember why two sacramental candles sit so beautifully and brightly on every altar. Every time Holy Communion is served, they remind you that Jesus Christ, true God and true man, miraculously gives you two things, His body and blood, with bread and wine. Jesus Christ comes to forgive you, renew you, and enlighten you every time He gives you not only just bread and wine but also His precious body and blood.

> Soul, adorn yourself with gladness,
> Leave the gloomy haunts of sadness,
> Come into the daylight's splendor,
> There with joy your praises render.
> Bless the One whose grace unbounded
> This amazing banquet founded;
> He, though heav'nly, high, and holy,
> Deigns to dwell with you most lowly (*LSB* 636:1).
> Amen.

Manna in the Desert

Read Exodus 16:1–2, 11–18

The eyes of all look to You, and You give them their
food in due season. You open Your hand; You satisfy
the desire of every living thing. (Psalm 145:15–16)

After God graciously delivered the people of Israel from the powers of Egypt and miraculously brought them through the Red Sea, the people still forgot God. The people grumbled at God and His leader, Moses, not just once but many times. Yet God heard their grumbling and provided manna every morning and quail every night.

Do you ever think, "Lord, I certainly need something different or more than this!" Well, your loving God still hears rebellious sinners and graciously sustains all people with daily bread, both the evil and the good (see Matthew 5:45). Jesus knows our forgetfulness, which is why He went to the rugged cross to shed His precious blood. Your heavenly Father promises to give you all you need and much more. As Jesus said, "Your heavenly Father knows that you need them all. But seek first the kingdom of God and His righteousness, and all these things will be added to you" (Matthew 6:32–33).

> Feed Thy children, God most holy;
> Comfort sinners poor and lowly.
> O Thou Bread of Life from heaven,
> Bless the food Thou here hast given!
> As these gifts the body nourish,
> May our souls in graces flourish
> Till with saints in heav'nly splendor
> At Thy feast due thanks we render (*LSB* 774). Amen.

LENT
WEEK FOUR

I Am the Bread of Life

Read John 6:35–59

Jesus said to them, "I am the bread of life; whoever
comes to Me shall not hunger, and whoever believes in
Me shall never thirst." (John 6:35)

After Jesus fed thousands, the Jews argued with Him. They even appealed to the greatness of their father Abraham (see John 8:39–47) and the prophet Moses see (John 6:32–37). However, they failed to see that Jesus Christ existed eternally before Abraham and that Abraham rejoiced to see Jesus' day (see John 8:56–58). Jesus also far exceeded Moses, who brought only the Law, while He brought grace and truth (see John 1:17; Hebrews 3:5–6).

Are you failing to see the greatness of your Savior? Are you hungering or longing for something more out of life outside of Jesus? Jesus Christ is the way, the truth, the life, and the very bread of life (see John 14:6). In Jesus, you will never hunger or thirst because He always refreshes, satisfies, and feeds every hungry and longing soul, especially yours. No one who comes to Him ever lacks anything or will be cast away. So partake of Him, eat His flesh, drink of His blood, and you will live forever.

> Lord Jesus Christ, life-giving bread,
> May I in grace possess You.
> Let me with holy food be fed,
> In hunger I address You.
> Prepare me well for You, O Lord,
> And, humbly by my prayer implored,
> Give me Your grace and mercy (*LSB* 625:1). Amen.

Eating the Same Spiritual Food

Read 1 Corinthians 10:1–5, 14–17

And all ate the same spiritual food, and all drank the
same spiritual drink. For they drank from the spiritual
Rock that followed them, and the Rock was Christ.
(1 Corinthians 10:3–4)

St. Paul commanded the Corinthians to avoid idol feasts and all sexual immorality. He made a direct spiritual application to the physical eating and drinking done in the wilderness by Israel, the people of God. Although all Israel ate the same food in the desert (manna) and drank (water) from the same spiritual Rock, it was not Moses who blessed, followed, and led them, but Jesus Christ, the Second Person of the Trinity! He was even the pillar of cloud by day and the pillar of fire at night throughout their forty years in the wilderness.

The Church today needs a Rock of refuge. That Rock is Jesus, the same one beaten for you, bloodied for you, and lifted on a cross for you. We eat spiritual food and drink from God's spiritual rock every time we receive the bread of life, Jesus, who gives His body in the bread and His blood through "the cup of blessing" (1 Corinthians 10:16).

> At the Lamb's high feast we sing
> Praise to our victorious King,
> Who has washed us in the tide
> Flowing from His pierced side. Alleluia!
>
> Praise we Christ, whose blood was shed,
> Paschal victim, paschal bread;
> With sincerity and love
> Eat we manna from above. Alleluia (*LSB* 633:1, 4)!
> Amen.

Sifted like Wheat

Read Mark 4:26–29

Simon, Simon, behold, Satan demanded to have you,
that he might sift you like wheat. (Luke 22:31)

To grow in faith during Lent is to be like wheat ground into flour. Each baptized child of God goes through many stages of faith maturity, but each day begins with being ground like grain. No one can avoid it. In order to make delicious bread, numerous wheat kernels must grow, mature, and also be ground up, separating the wheat from the chaff.

As members of Christ's Body, His Church, each day we are being sifted and milled through the threshing floor of life, which includes suffering, pain, temptations, and repentance. Jesus was ground down as well, bearing all your sin on His cross. Peter also was sifted like wheat. Until your earthly life ends, the chaff of your sinful nature must be ground up and crucified so that a new man, like new wheat, may rise to become a full loaf in Christ. The Holy Spirit continues His good work in you and each member of His Church so that all of us become one united loaf, the Body of Christ for this world.

> Lord Jesus, although I am sifted like wheat, as St. Peter
> was through temptation, denial, trials, and repentance,
> help me never lose hope, peace, or faith in You, the
> bread of life and my eternal Savior. Amen.

Give Us This Day Our Daily Bread

Read Luke 11:1–13

Which of you who has a friend will go to him at midnight and say to him, "Friend, lend me three loaves, for a friend of mine has arrived on a journey, and I have nothing to set before him." (Luke 11:5–6)

When the disciples asked Jesus to teach them to pray, He led them through the Lord's Prayer (see Luke 11:2–4). Dr. Martin Luther says that every morning when we get up, or each evening before we go to bed, we should make the sign of the cross over our hearts and then repeat the Apostles' Creed and the Lord's Prayer. The Lord's Prayer includes a summary of who God is as well as what we need most, especially daily food and forgiveness. We pray the Lord's Prayer often because it always reminds us of the source of our daily bread.

On every Lord's Day, Sunday, we pray the Lord's Prayer when the Sacrament of Holy Communion is offered. It is placed here, near the Words of Institution, to remind you of the bread of life you need to eat the most, which is offered at this Holy Table. Jesus is manna and bread for your soul.

> I come, O Savior, to Thy table,
> For weak and weary is my soul;
> Thou, Bread of Life, alone art able
> To satisfy and make me whole:
> Lord, may Thy body and Thy blood
> Be for my soul the highest good (*LSB* 618:1)! Amen.

Sweeter Than Honey

Read Psalm 19

How sweet are Your words to my taste,
sweeter than honey to my mouth! (Psalm 119:103)

Just as God created the world and all things in heaven and on earth with His voice, so God still sustains, refreshes, and instills life. King David beautifully describes God's Word as perfect, reviving, sure, right, pure, true, and more precious than gold (Psalm 19:7–10). His Word is edible, exactly like bread or food for the soul. God's Word is sweeter than honey, more satisfying, and more precious than any gold in this world.

That is why we treasure the Word of God through which all things came. It is a Means of Grace, whereby God's mercy, love, and forgiveness flow directly through our ears and into our hearts and minds. It always satisfies because His Word always centers on His Son, Jesus Christ, who was with God in the beginning and is God (see John 1:1). This Word made flesh, born of the Virgin Mary, who suffered under Pontius Pilate, came to save you. He even still gives His flesh for you. Yes, His Word is sweeter than honey from a honeycomb and is manna for your soul, now and forever.

How sweet the name of Jesus sounds
In a believer's ear!
It soothes our sorrows, heals our wounds,
And drives away our fear.

It makes the wounded spirit whole
And calms the heart's unrest;
'Tis manna to the hungry soul
And to the weary, rest (*LSB* 524:1–2). Amen.

Palms and Victory

Read John 12:9–19

Rejoice greatly, O daughter of Zion! Shout aloud, O daughter of Jerusalem! Behold, your king is coming to you; righteous and having salvation is He.

(Zechariah 9:9)

Palm branches were often a symbol of victory, joy, life, and peace in the Scriptures (see Deuteronomy 34:3; 1 Kings 6:32–35; Psalm 92; Ezekiel 41:18; Song of Songs 7:7; Revelation 7:9). They were the chief feature of the ancient Feast of Tabernacles, celebrated victoriously and annually by Israel because God provided all that the people of God needed in the wilderness for forty years (see Leviticus 23:40). Later, Jesus raised Lazarus from the dead in the town of Bethany, and the news spread rapidly. Therefore, when Jesus entered Jerusalem for Passover, palms were waving before Him as King. Jesus is your Messiah, victory, hope, peace, and comfort, now and always. It may not have seemed like Jesus was victorious when they placed a purple robe on Him, punched Him, and set a crown of thorns on His head. However, make no mistake about it: your King endured all this to give you rest and an eternal victory! He licked up the dust of His humility (see Psalm 22:15), bore your sins, and conquered whatever the devil threw at Him to give you peace now and forever.

> Ride on, ride on in majesty!
> Hark! All the tribes hosanna cry.
> O Savior meek, pursue Thy road,
> With palms and scattered garments strowed.
>
> Ride on, ride on in majesty!
> In lowly pomp ride on to die.
> O Christ, Thy triumphs now begin
> O'er captive death and conquered sin (*LSB* 441:1–2).
> Amen.

From Palms to Ashes

Read Luke 19:37–44

My strength is dried up like a potsherd, and my tongue
sticks to my jaws; You lay me in the dust of death.

(Psalm 22:15)

It is a common practice among congregations to save the palm branches from Palm Sunday and then burn the dried-out palms to make ashes for the next year's Ash Wednesday. This creates a cycle, going from joy to repentance. When Jesus entered Jerusalem from the east, descending the Mount of Olives, people joyously threw cloaks down, raised palm branches, and cried, "Blessed is the King who comes in the name of the Lord! Peace in heaven and glory in the highest" (Luke 19:38). However, while some rejoiced, the Pharisees and most of Jerusalem rejected Him. He desired to gather all people under His wing like a mother hen does her chicks, but they would not (see Matthew 23:37).

As Holy Week approaches, are you lifting up palms or wailing in ashes? What kind of Jesus are you seeking? A miracle worker to just make life now better? Seek Jesus, your King sent to save you, who conquers the devil, sin, and death! Cast all your sins and iniquities on Him, and you will have peace now and life forever.

Lord Jesus, think on me
And purge away my sin;
From worldly passions set me free
And make me pure within.

Lord Jesus, think on me
That, when this life is past,
I may the eternal brightness see
And share Your joy at last (*LSB* 610: 1, 5). Amen.

LENT
WEEK FIVE

Realizing You Are Naked

Read Genesis 3:1–11

And a young man followed Him, with nothing but a
linen cloth about his body. And they seized him, but he
left the linen cloth and ran away naked. (Mark 14:51–52)

When my sons were little, my wife and I often bathed them together. Afterward, it was not uncommon for one boy to slip out of his towel and sprint down the hallway, cheerfully yelling, "*Naked* boys!" This, however, was not Adam and Eve's reaction after they sinned. They immediately recognized good and evil. Now naked, they were ashamed, sewed fig leaves together, and hid from God (see Genesis 3:7–8). But in spite of this, God still walked toward them, calling, "Where are you?" (Genesis 3:9). Further, He covered them with new garments of skin after He promised to redeem them through the seed of the woman (see Genesis 3:15, 21). Your Baptism strips you naked every day. "Put off your old self," says St. Paul, and "put on the new" (Ephesians 4:22–24). The second Adam, Jesus, unlike the first Adam, hangs naked on a cross for you. He still calls you today: "Come to Me, all who labor and are heavy laden, and I will give you rest" (Matthew 11:28). Clothed anew in the white robe of Christ's righteousness in Holy Baptism, your nakedness and sin are all covered!

> Nothing in my hand I bring;
> Simply to Thy cross I cling.
> Naked, come to Thee for dress;
> Helpless, look to Thee for grace;
> Foul, I to the fountain fly;
> Wash me, Savior, or I die (*LSB* 761:3). Amen.

Stripped Naked

Read Matthew 27:27–37

And they stripped Him and put a scarlet robe on
Him. . . . And when they had crucified Him, they
divided His garments among them by casting lots.
(Matthew 27:28, 35)

When Jesus was crucified, He was publicly mocked before both Jews and Gentiles. All open shame was placed on Him. However, eventually, He set it all aside, "nailing it to the cross" (Colossians 2:14), and overcame death and the grave by rising again. After new adult Christians in the Early Church were fully instructed in the faith, they were invited by their sponsor to strip out of their old clothing for Baptism on Easter Vigil. After entering the baptismal pool naked, they were immersed three times. But after they exited, they wore a new, white robe.[3] In this way, all baptized Christians imitate their Lord who was stripped naked, but they are clothed anew. Stripping off the old clothes of sin through repentance is still a daily practice for all the baptized before they rise again with Christ. We say in our baptismal rite, "Receive this white garment to show that you have been clothed with the robe of Christ's righteousness that covers all your sin" (*LSB*, p. 271). Since you are clothed in Jesus, in His grace, forgiveness, and love, you stand not in shame but in honor before the Father, reflecting peace and hope wherever you go (Matthew 5:14).

> In a wat'ry grave are buried
> All our sins that Jesus carried;
> Christ, the Ark of Life, has ferried
> Us across death's raging flood (*LSB* 597:2). Amen.

---

3   Thomas M. Finn, *Early Christian Baptism and the Catechumenate: West and East Syria* (Collegeville, MN: Michael Glazier and The Liturgical Press, 1992) 5:8.

Once Naked, Now Clothed

Read Colossians 3:1–17

As he came from his mother's womb he shall go again,
naked as he came, and shall take nothing for his toil
that he may carry away in his hand. (Ecclesiastes 5:15)

King Solomon proclaims a parallel: just as you were born naked, you will die naked, taking nothing with you. Job even concurs with this (see Job 1:21). Jesus Christ was not naked when He existed eternally as the Second Person of the Trinity. However, He humbled Himself, was conceived by the Holy Spirit, and was born of Mary in time, naked, in Bethlehem. Later, our Lord was even embarrassingly stripped before being nailed to a cross. However, even while Roman soldiers bartered for His clothes, your salvation was never in jeopardy. Jesus went to the cross to kill the power of sin, death, and hell for you. Now you are hidden and blanketed in Jesus before God who will judge the living and the dead (see Hebrews 4:13). In Jesus, you have new white clothes of compassion, kindness, and patience that will never wear out, washed in the blood of the Lamb (Revelation 7:13–14). This is why everyone who is baptized is given a white cloth to remind them that they are now clothed in Jesus and all His righteousness.

> Jesus, Thy blood and righteousness
> My beauty are, my glorious dress;
> Midst flaming worlds, in these arrayed,
> With joy shall I lift up my head (*LSB* 563:1). Amen.

Anointed in Baptism

Read Luke 4:16–21

And [Moses] poured some of the anointing oil on
Aaron's head and anointed him to consecrate him.
(Leviticus 8:12)

Oil was often used to anoint various objects, utensils, and people in the Old Testament. Jacob anointed the rock at Bethel twice after God blessed him, gave him the land of Canaan, and promised to make his family numerous (see Genesis 28:18; 35:14). Later, Moses anointed Aaron as priest to set him apart as the high priest. The prophet Samuel anointed King Saul and King David as well, setting them apart for their tasks (see 1 Samuel 10:1; 16:13). Finally, after Jesus' Baptism by John the Baptist in the Jordan River (see Luke 3) and temptation by the devil (see Luke 4:1–13), Jesus entered His hometown of Nazareth, proclaiming, "The Spirit of the Lord is upon Me, because He has anointed Me to proclaim good news to the poor" (Luke 4:18). You are sealed and anointed by the Holy Spirit too (see Ephesians 1:14)! God has set you apart for service in this world. God's seal was placed on you through water and the Word, redeeming and washing you in the blood of Christ. Now, as His child, you reflect the light of Christ with joy, knowing your purpose for life.

> Baptized into Your name most holy,
> O Father, Son, and Holy Ghost,
> I claim a place, though weak and lowly,
> Among Your saints, Your chosen host.
> Buried with Christ and dead to sin,
> Your Spirit now shall live within (*LSB* 590:1). Amen.

Look Out, Not Within

Read 1 Peter 1:3–9

For I know that my Redeemer lives, and at the last
He will stand upon the earth. And after my skin has
been thus destroyed, yet in my flesh I shall see God.
(Job 19:25–26)

After most of Job's life and possessions were stripped away, his wife said to him, "Do you still hold fast your integrity? Curse God and die" (Job 2:9). God often uses trial and sufferings to refine faith, the same way gold or silver is refined. Other people may even chime in on the attack, making you lose heart and feel that life is all for nothing.

Lent calls you to reflect again on the real inherited nature of your sinful being. However, Lent is not a time to pout, grumble, or complain. Faith calls you to look outside yourself, to trust in God's promises in His Word, and to look to His Son, Jesus Christ. Gaze beyond life's ashes and remember you are baptized into Jesus Christ, who bore all sufferings for you by His sacrificial and loving death on the cross! Since Jesus rose again, slaughtering death's power and grip, you rise to new life every day, even in the midst of trials.

> Savior, when in dust to Thee
> Low we bow the adoring knee;
> When, repentant, to the skies
> Scarce we lift our weeping eyes;
> O, by all Thy pains and woe
> Suffered once for us below,
> Bending from Thy throne on high,
> Hear our penitential cry (*LSB* 419:1)! Amen.

Jesus: Closer than Ever

Read Ephesians 1:15–23

He who descended is the one who also ascended far
above all the heavens, that He might fill all things.
(Ephesians 4:10)

A professor once told me, "Don't put God in a box!" Far too often, we minimize a mystery rather than believe it! Even though St. Paul clearly states that Jesus Christ, our risen and ascended King, "fills all in all" and that "all things [are] under His feet," we assume that He is not physically present everywhere with His physical flesh. Listen again: Jesus Christ is the Head over His Body, the Church, "the fullness of Him who fills all in all" (Ephesians 1:22–23).

As we approach Holy Week, ponder all the wealth God gives you through His eternal Son! Jesus is not bound to a chair or throne in heaven. To "sit at the right hand of God" means that Jesus has all authority in heaven and on earth, filling the entire universe with both divine and human natures. Since your Lord died on the cross, rose from the tomb, and ascended to heaven, your salvation is complete. Now He still feeds the Church His true body and blood. Therefore, Jesus is wonderfully closer to you than you could ever imagine!

> Though reason cannot understand,
> Yet faith this truth embraces:
> Your body, Lord, is even now
> At once in many places.
> I leave to You how this can be;
> Your Word alone suffices me;
> I trust its truth unfailing (*LSB* 622:5). Amen.

The Old Rugged Cross

Read Psalm 22

And you, who were dead in your trespasses . . . , God
made alive together with Him, having forgiven us all
our trespasses, by canceling the record of debt that
stood against us. . . . This He set aside, nailing it to the
cross. (Colossians 2:13–14)

Psalm 22 is usually read at the end of the Holy Thursday service as the altar, lectern, and pulpit are stripped. As colorful paraments are removed, bare wood remains. Wood has a long history in the Bible. It reminds us about what took place on the tree at Golgotha where our Lord once died. This Holy Week, we highlight both the old rugged cross and its close counterpart, water. Noah built a wooden ark to save his family of eight and numerous animals from the watery flood. Moses threw a log of wood into the bitter waters of Marah to sweeten them. Finally, Elisha used a wooden stick to make an iron axe head float so it could be retrieved from the Jordan River. These images of wood with water are not accidental; they are crucial to understanding the depth and width of God's salvation at the cross and through Holy Baptism. Jesus uplifts sinners, raises the dead, and sweetens all sour experiences through His cross and your Baptism. Jesus Christ is your refuge, lifesaver, and rock, now and forever!

In the cross of Christ I glory,
Tow'ring o'er the wrecks of time.
All the light of sacred story
Gathers round its head sublime (*LSB* 427:1). Amen.

HOLY WEEK

Wood That Rescues

Read Genesis 6

Baptism, which corresponds to this [Noah and family being saved through water], now saves you, not as a removal of dirt from the body but as an appeal to God for a good conscience, through the resurrection of Jesus Christ. (1 Peter 3:21)

God could have chosen many other ways to save Noah and his family from a flood, but He did not. Instead, God instructed Noah to build a wooden boat, an ark, to keep his entire family and all land animals safe. God rescued them, floating them above a raging flood. When St. Peter refers to this, he connects it to how Baptism saves you. Baptism is intimately connected to Jesus' death on the cross, burial, and resurrection. Since you died with Jesus, you are also raised with Him every day (see Romans 6).

Do any floods overwhelm you now? Are you drowning in family troubles, relational misunderstandings, or other hardships? Amid any troubled waters, the "wood" of Christ's cross keeps you afloat, rescuing you from all your distresses (see Psalm 34). Since Jesus allowed the entire weight and guilt of sin from all to flood onto Him, it no longer drowns or disturbs you. Instead, He permitted Himself to be "forsaken" by the Father (Matthew 27:46). Let His cross always remind you how it rescues you, now and always!

> When the woes of life o'ertake me,
> Hopes deceive, and fears annoy,
> Never shall the cross forsake me;
> Lo, it glows with peace and joy (*LSB* 427:2). Amen.

Wood That Sweetens

Read Exodus 15:22–27

And he cried to the LORD, and the LORD showed him
a log, and he threw it into the water, and the water
became sweet. (Exodus 15:25)

After Israel was baptized in the Red Sea and walked on dry land, the Egyptian army was drowned (see Exodus 14:26–30; 1 Corinthians 10:2). Following this, the people of God sang the Song of Moses, praising God for His deliverance. However, three days later, these same forgetful people were grumbling and crying for water in the wilderness. God heard Moses' prayer and showed him a wooden log. When Moses threw it into the bitter waters at Marah, they miraculously became sweet and drinkable again!

God did not choose to have Moses speak to the water or place his staff in it. Instead, God told Moses to throw a wooden log into those bitter waters. Sometimes we remember God's provision, promises, and forgiveness, but at other times, we forget and grumble. If you feel like you are suffering and swallowing some bitter pills in life, do not become embittered by them! Rather, know that God works good through all of them so that you trust in Him (see Romans 8:28). He never leaves you, and He promises to sweeten your life through the wood of Christ's cross, which forgives all of your sins and eases every pain and burden.

> When the sun of bliss is beaming
> Light and love upon my way,
> From the cross the radiance streaming
> Adds more luster to the day (*LSB* 427:3). Amen.

Wood That Lightens

Read 2 Kings 6:1–7

For He will hide me in His shelter in the day of trouble;
He will conceal me under the cover of His tent; He will
lift me high upon a rock. (Psalm 27:5)

When the prophets were intending to construct a larger place of lodging, they were cutting down trees, which grew abundantly near the Jordan River. However, they had an accident. One of the prophets was using a borrowed axe when the iron axe head flew off the wood handle and sank to the bottom of the river. After Elisha became aware of this, he cut off a stick and threw the piece of wood into the river, and suddenly, the heavy iron axe head floated and was retrieved.

This miracle with wood completely opposed the natural laws of gravity. God does the same for you, promising to raise you up out of any of life's seeming impossibilities. The wood of Christ's cross opposes gravity, raises you up, and forgives all of your sins. Baptized into Christ and His death and resurrection, your life is lifted up now and forever. In Holy Baptism, you are raised with Christ because He rose from the dead. No circumstance of life, however great the sin or trouble, will ever weigh you down forever because Jesus Christ always lifts you up.

> Bane and blessing, pain and pleasure
> By the cross are sanctified;
> Peace is there that knows no measure,
> Joys that through all time abide (*LSB* 427:4). Amen.

Strike the Rock

Read John 19:28–37

Behold, I will stand before you there on the rock at
Horeb, and you shall strike the rock, and water shall
come out of it, and the people will drink. (Exodus 17:6)

Although Israel often grumbled against Moses and God, God never left them empty-handed. God either graciously sweetened existing bitter water (see Exodus 15:25) or brought water out of a lifeless rock. This is why Jesus said, "Therefore do not be anxious, saying, 'What shall we eat?' or 'What shall we drink? . . . Your heavenly Father knows that you need them all. But seek first the kingdom of God" (Matthew 6:31–33). Grumbling results from our faithless human nature, which even Moses displayed, striking the rock twice in frustration with Israel, thus making him forfeit entering the Promised Land.

Unlike Moses, who struck a rock with his staff to bring forth water, your eternal rock, Jesus, allowed His body to be stricken with a spear by a Roman soldier. From Jesus' side, water and blood still flow for us (see 1 John 5:6). Baptismal water cleanses, and living water quenches thirsty souls. His holy blood also washes away all sin for those who come to His Supper. If anyone drinks of Jesus, trusting in Him, he will never thirst. Out of his heart will flow living water (see John 7:37–38).

Heavenly Father, crucify my grumbling flesh so that as
Your baptized child, I may always thirst for Jesus, the
living water for eternal life. In Jesus' name. Amen.

Water, Blood, and Spirit

Read 1 John 5:5–12

One of the soldiers pierced His side with a spear, and at
once there came out blood and water. (John 19:34)

The Jews asked Pilate to take the bodies down from their crosses
so that they would not be hanging there over the Sabbath Day. St.
John is the only Gospel writer to acknowledge that after the Roman
soldiers broke the legs of the first two criminals, they did not break
the legs of our Lord since it was evident that Jesus was already dead.
One soldier took the tip of his spear and pierced it into Jesus' side,
causing blood and water to gush forth. These actions fulfilled two
Old Testament prophecies. First, not one of Jesus' bones was broken
(Psalm 34:20; 22:17); second, the Jews would look at the one they
had pierced (Zechariah 12:10).

St. John adds later that three witnesses—the water, the blood,
and the Spirit—all testify and all agree that Jesus Christ is the Lord of
Life. The water pouring out from Jesus' side refers to Holy Baptism,
and the blood corresponds to what Jesus gives in His own Supper.
This Holy Thursday, remember the bounteous gift Jesus still gives as
part of His last will and testament—His Holy Supper—and joyously
receive it now and always!

> Water, blood, and Spirit crying,
> By their witness testifying
> To the One whose death-defying
> Life has come, with life for all (*LSB* 597:1). Amen.

What Do You Smell Like?

Read 2 Corinthians 2:12–17

When the LORD smelled the pleasing aroma, the LORD
said in His heart, "I will never again curse the ground
because of man, for the intention of man's heart is evil
from his youth." (Genesis 8:21)

What is the best fragrance to imagine? A fresh pan of chocolate chip cookies? A dozen fresh red roses? How about the bouquet of a red Cabernet wine aged well? What about the smell of beautiful Easter lilies on Easter morning? All are beautiful fragrances, leaving an indelible mark on your memory. After Noah made his sacrifice following the flood, God was pleased with the aroma, promising never to curse the ground again.

How do you smell? St. Paul told the Corinthian Christians that he was a pleasing aroma to those who believe and the aroma of death to those who do not believe. Do you always pass the "stench test" with your spouse, children, and friends? No, we often stink! However, washed and baptized into Jesus Christ every day and anointed with Him, we smell fresh every day. Your life is different! Fragrant oil reminds baptized Christians that they are sweet and pleasing to God, washed and forgiven through Jesus Christ, who was offered on the cross for you!

This flow'r, whose fragrance tender
With sweetness fills the air,
Dispels with glorious splendor
The darkness ev'rywhere.
True man, yet very God,
From sin and death He saves us
And lightens ev'ry load (*LSB* 359:3). Amen.

On the Verge of Jordan (the Promised Land)

Read Joshua 3

Oh, give thanks to the LORD, for He is good, for this steadfast love endures forever! Let the redeemed of the LORD say so, whom He has redeemed from trouble.
(Psalm 107:1–2)

A family trip or family reunion requires much planning. A desirable location must be selected, acceptable dates must be chosen to accommodate family schedules, and good lodging must be reserved. Although Moses planned for more than forty years to enter the Promised Land, he did not do so. But Joshua did. The themes of failure, sin, and rebellion are plentiful in the history of Israel. They wandered for forty years before Joshua, by God's grace, brought them across the Jordan River and into the Promised Land.

Today, we look forward to entering our promised land of Easter. Jesus, your greater Joshua, entered the swelling Jordan River, conquering death forever on the cross. You have waited all Lent for Easter, the joyous celebration of Jesus Christ's resurrection from the dead. Come and celebrate! We are ready to meet, eat, and rest in the resurrected Lord Jesus. He is risen! He is risen indeed! Alleluia!

> Death's flood has lost its chill
> Since Jesus crossed the river;
> Lover of souls, from ill
> My passing soul deliver:
> Had Christ, who once was slain,
> Not burst His three-day prison,
> Our faith had been in vain:
> But now has Christ arisen, arisen, arisen;
> But now has Christ arisen (*LSB* 482:2)! Amen.

The Feast of All Feasts

Read Isaiah 55:1–5

On the mountain the Lord of hosts will make for all
peoples a feast of rich food, a feast of well-aged wine,
of rich food full of marrow. . . . He will swallow up on
this mountain the covering that is cast over all peoples.
. . . He will swallow up death forever. (Isaiah 25:6–8)

Themes of feasting often describe the beauty of eternal life with God. Isaiah emphasizes that God's people will be enjoying an eternal heavenly feast on God's holy mountain. This is why the Church often sings "This Is the Feast" (*LSB*, p. 155) during the Divine Service as we anticipate feasting on God's Word (see Psalm 19:7–10) and receiving the Lord's Supper. The Promised Land was often described as a good and gracious land overflowing with milk and honey. Heaven is like that too. Jesus describes it in His parable of the wedding feast (see Matthew 22:1–14). On this holy day, the first communicants not only received the body and blood of Christ but also a glass of milk mixed with honey. Remember, you have crossed over from death to life! In the Lord's Supper, you are partaking of the promised land of heaven, and you are getting a glimpse of heaven at the Lamb's high feast.

> At the Lamb's high feast we sing
> Praise to our victorious King,
> Who has washed us in the tide
> Flowing from His pierced side. Alleluia!
>
> Praise we Him, whose love divine
> Gives His sacred blood for wine,
> Gives His body for the feast—
> Christ the victim, Christ the priest. Alleluia(*LSB*
> 633:1–2)! Amen.